THE GOODEN FAMILY LEARNS TOGETHER

BY

ROBYNN RENO

Published by
Blessed Hope Publishers
Hagerstown, Md.

Publishing and Formatting Assisted by
The Old Paths Publications
142 Gold Flume Way
Cleveland, GA 30528
Web address: www.theoldpathspublications.com
Email address: TOP@theoldpathspublications.com

Illustrations by: Benjamin Gamonal. The cover has been designed using images from freepik.com

All Scripture quotations in this book are taken from the King James Version of the Bible.
"All scripture is given by inspiration of God, and is profitable for doctrine, for reproof, for correction, for instruction in righteousness. That the man of God may be perfect, throughly furnished unto all good works." **(II Tim. 3:16, 17)**

<u>DEDICATION</u>

This work is dedicated to Pastor Paul Reno, my father, and his wife, Carolyn, my mother, who are the true inspirations behind the Gooden family. I am so blessed to have been raised by you. God knew exactly who I needed for parents! I love you!!

TABLE OF CONTENTS

DEDICATION 3

TABLE OF CONTENTS 5

The Gooden Family 7

Chapter 1: The Gooden Family Learns About the Deaf 9

Chapter 2: The Gooden Family Helps Widows 13

Chapter 3: The Gooden Family Learns About Autism 17

Chapter 4: The Gooden Family Learns About Adoption 21

Chapter 5: The Gooden Family Learns About the Blind 25

Chapter 6: The Gooden Family Gives Their Best 29

Chapter 7 The Gooden Family and Father´s Day 33

Chapter 8: The Gooden Family Learns About Death 37

Chapter 9: The Gooden Family Celebrates Thanksgiving 41

Chapter 10: The Gooden Family Shares Their Dreams 45

ABOUT THE AUTHOR 49

The Gooden Family

Mr. Gooden – Father and husband, he also pastors a small church and has a burden to raise his children so they will serve the Lord.

Mrs. Gooden – A very loving wife and devoted mother of five. She keeps the household moving smoothly and often stays home with the children while her pastor husband takes mission trips.

Beth – The oldest child. Beth is 16 and very sensitive to others´ feelings. She is an obedient daughter and works hard to help her mother with household chores and the younger children, especially Joanna.

Sue – The second daughter, Sue is the one who keeps the family laughing. She is 14 years old and quite a tomboy. Her best friend is her sister Beth.

Paul – The middle child and oldest son, at 12 years old, Paul carries the load of helping his Dad with the outside chores. He has a giving heart and works hard to help others.

Joanna – The youngest daughter of the Gooden children. She is an inquisitive, animated young lady who looks much older than her 9 years.

Tommy – The youngest of the Gooden children. He is an active 6 year old who enjoys sports and is mischievous but has a soft heart.

Chapter 1

The Gooden Family Learns About the Deaf

"Joanna, telephone!" Mrs. Gooden called.

Joanna bounded into the kitchen excited to have someone call her. She took the phone with wide eyes and a huge smile.

"Hello…yes, it is. Yes, I remember…ok…really? Wow! Thank you so much! … I understand…two weeks…yes…I will do my best…ok…thank you so much for the opportunity! … right, ok, bye bye!"

As Joanna hung up the phone she jumped up and down and squealed with delight. Mrs. Gooden waited patiently for her to explain what had just happened.

"Mom! I can´t believe it!! I was chosen to write an article for the children´s section of the newspaper. Can you believe it? Oh my…what topic should I choose? I want to learn about so many things…it is so hard to pick just one."

"Well dear, you can certainly learn new things whether you write an article about them or not. But I have an idea for you. Do you remember last week when we were at Tommy´s game and we saw those deaf people talking to each other? You seemed intrigued with that, why don´t we do some research and see if you can talk to someone who can hear, but knows sign language?" Mrs. Gooden said.

"Great idea, Mom. I will do that as soon as I finish vacuuming."

Before long Joanna was typing away on the computer, trying to find information about the deaf. She found one site that showed the hand positions for the letters of the alphabet, and began trying to do each one. She also found many videos that people had posted explaining how to communicate with the deaf. But what she really wanted was to talk to someone and ask some questions. She decided to search the web to see if any nearby churches had ministries to the deaf. Right away she found a church which did and made a phone call to get more information. She left her phone number and asked the secretary to pass it on to the person involved in the deaf ministry.

A few days later the phone rang and once again someone wanted to talk to Joanna. It was Mrs. Patty, the lady who worked in her church´s deaf ministry and she agreed to meet Joanna at a nearby park so they could talk about the deaf. Joanna was so excited. She bounced around the house, doing her chores and her research until it was time to go to the park for the interview.

"Mrs. Patty," Joanna began, "what made you want to learn sign language? It must be hard to learn a new language."

"Well, as a child I knew there were deaf people in the world, but I didn´t know any so I didn´t really think about how they would communicate. And then, when my daughter was in school she studied about sign language and I became a little more interested. Then, one day in church the Pastor was preaching from Mark 16:15 and he really emphasized the word *every*. 'Go ye into all the world and preach the gospel to *every* creature.' And that made me think of the deaf people. Who was telling them about the gospel? I knew that there were deaf people in our city and that it was our responsibility to tell them about Jesus. So, I went to college and learned how to sign. Now I interpret the messages at church."

"Oh my, that is so neat. I never thought about that before. And you can explain to someone that can´t hear anything how they can go to heaven?" Joanna inquired.

"I sure can. It is the greatest privilege I have, to be able to share about Jesus," Mrs. Patty replied.

"Well, that would take a long time to learn, but would you please teach me how to do a few signs?" Joanna continued.

"Sure. To say *hello* you can either wave or do a salute. The salute is the more formal way to greet someone."

Joanna tried the sign both ways.

"If you want to ask *how are you?* you cup your hand with the thumb sticking up, start at the level of your chest and roll it out and then point at the person. The hand position for the word *how* is called the '5 hand shape bent'. Do you want to try that?"

This sign was a bit harder, but soon Joanna was able to do it.

"And then if you want to say *goodbye* you can just wave like a little child," Mrs. Patty finished.

Joanna practiced each sign several times before thanking Mrs. Patty for taking the time to chat with her.

"Thank you for meeting me and helping me today. I will be praying for you, that God will help you share the gospel with many deaf people," Joanna said. "And, who knows, maybe some day I will be a missionary, and learn a new language so I can tell others about Jesus, too."

Chapter 2

The Gooden Family Helps Widows

As the Gooden family gathered in their living room for family devotions, Paul seemed a bit sad.

"Please don´t worry about it," Sue said, "we will figure something out."

"Why is Paul sad and worried?" Joanna asked.

"I haven´t been able to find enough ways to earn money and I need to give my offering to Faith Promise for our missionaries," Paul replied.

"Well, son, tonight in devotions we will look at a few verses that might give you some ideas," Mr. Gooden said quietly.

After they sang a few songs, Mr. Gooden opened his Bible and began to speak. "I am going to read a verse from James, chapter one. Verse twenty-seven says, 'Pure religion and undefiled before God and the Father is this, To visit the fatherless and widows in their affliction, and to keep himself unspotted from the world.' So we see that God says we need to visit, or help, the fatherless and widows and keep ourselves unspotted from the world. Tonight we are going to talk about how we can help the fatherless and widows. Does anyone have any ideas?"

"I noticed as I came home from the grocery store today that the bushes at Mrs. Cross´ house need trimming," Mrs. Gooden replied.

"Good idea, she is a widow and certainly doesn´t have the strength to do that job. If she tried, she could fall and get hurt!" Mr. Gooden added. "Paul, you did a good job trimming our bushes, would you like to offer to help Mrs. Cross?"

Paul was not very enthusiastic but he agreed that he could try to help. Mrs. Cross was not a favorite neighbor, with her fussy attitude. But Paul knew that helping her would please the Lord so he was willing to do it.

"But Dad, we all know that she won´t pay Paul no matter how hard he works or how good of a job he does. That lady must be Scrooge´s sister!" Sue exclaimed.

After everyone finished laughing Mr. Gooden answered Sue, "What we need to remember is that sometimes we do things just because it is the right thing, not expecting any payment. But also remember that Proverbs 14:23a says, 'In all labour there is profit...' so we know that somehow, some way the Lord will make sure that Paul profits from his work. It may be that he learns something new that will help him in a future job, we just don´t know. But we do know that the Lord keeps His word and also that He wants us to help widows.”

As the family prayed together, each one remembered to ask the Lord to help Paul earn the money he needed, but also that He help them to remember to look for ways to help the widows.

The next day was Saturday, so after cleaning his room and doing his chores, Paul set out to visit the widow, Mrs. Cross. He was gone for quite a long time but when he returned for lunch he had a huge smile on his face. After asking the Lord´s blessing on the lunch Mr. Gooden asked Paul why he was so happy.

“Wow, Dad, today was AWESOME! You know I wasn´t all that excited about helping Mrs. Cross and sure enough she was her normal self, living up to her name. But I kept thinking about that verse in Proverbs so I asked the Lord to help me see some area of profit in helping her, because I wasn´t learning anything new. Anyway, as I finished trimming her bushes she told me to sweep her sidewalks and driveway. And that is when it happened!”

“What happened?” Tommy asked. The whole family was so eager to hear about Paul´s morning that nobody had even started to eat.

"Well, her neighbor must have seen me working and he came and asked me to mow his lawn for him. And he PAID me – exactly what I need to give to the missionary program at church. AND he wants me to mow for the whole summer! So even though Mrs. Cross didn´t pay me the Lord made sure that I would profit from that work."

"Oh my, that is incredible," said Joanna. "We need to pray again and thank the Lord for answering our prayer."

And that is exactly what they did.

Chapter 3

The Gooden Family Learns About Autism

Mrs. Gooden had the habit of getting up early every morning so that she could read her Bible and pray before the day really got started and she needed to care for her husband and children. On this particular morning she had reached 1 Thessalonians chapter five in her reading. Verse fourteen especially caught her attention, "Now we exhort you, brethren, warn them that are unruly, comfort the feebleminded, support the weak, be patient toward all men." She reread this verse several times, asking the Lord to help her recognize the different types of people and react in a godly fashion to them.

As she made breakfast for her family and got the children off to school she kept going over the verse in her mind, knowing that the Lord had something special for her that day.

After lunch, Mrs. Gooden headed out to run errands and get groceries. As she pushed her cart through the store she passed, several times, a young mother and her little boy. She realized that, though the mother chatted with her son, the little boy never answered, choosing rather to do odd things with his fingers and make grunting sounds. The young mother wasn't frustrated with

her son, but Mrs. Gooden could tell she was very tired.

Remembering her verse from that morning Mrs. Gooden decided to try to speak to the young mother and her son. "Are you helping your mother do some shopping?" she asked the next time she passed them.

"This is my son, Manassie," the mother replied, "he is autistic and non-verbal. But he will give you high five or shake your hand and he loves hugs."

"Well, I love hugs too," stated Mrs. Gooden as she leaned over and gave the sweet boy a hug. "What is your name and how old is Manassie?" she asked the mother.

"I am Cristie and Manassie is four."

"Well, I have a six year old at home that loves to go to the park on a nice day. Do you think that you and Manassie would like to meet my son and me at a park and see if he will play with Tommy? I know each autistic child is different but if he would enjoy that, I know my son will treat him as you suggest."

Tears filled Cristie's eyes at the kindness Mrs. Gooden was showing her. "Yes, I would love to meet you and your son at the park. As long as Tommy understands that Manassie may just want to run around and flap his hands rather than get on the playground equipment we will be fine. I will stay close by in case he needs me, but some adult conversation will be welcome. How about Saturday morning at City Park?"

"That will be great. How about 10:00?" Mrs. Gooden answered.

Soon the mothers said good bye and continued their grocery shopping. Mrs. Gooden was grateful for the opportunity to encourage a young mother and also to allow her to have a little break while their sons played together.

When Tommy arrived home from school Mrs. Gooden sat down with him to explain about Manassie. She explained that he needed to be kind and understanding because Manassie would have reactions that are different than other children. She talked to Tommy about her verse and explained that this was an opportunity for him to be patient.

Saturday morning was sunny and warm. As soon as Manassie saw Tommy he ran right to him and gave him a hug. Tommy remembered that Manassie didn't speak so he took his hand and led him over to the slide. Soon Manassie was running around and flapping his hands, happy as he could be. The other children at the park were looking at him strangely. Several of them made comments so Tommy went and spoke to them.

"My new friend Manassie has autism and he has reactions that are different to yours and mine. That doesn't make them wrong – just different. We need to be patient with him" he explained.

The other children began to share that they had classmates who had autism and began to run around and flap their hands with Manassie.

Before the boys were ready the mothers called them to leave. Several of the other children came over to hug Manassie good bye and invite him to come back another day.

Tommy and Mrs. Gooden headed home knowing the Lord had taught them so many new things through this experience.

Chapter 4

The Gooden Family Learns About Adoption

The Gooden family had just finished thanking the Lord for their supper when Beth, the oldest daughter, said, "Mom, why do people have to be adopted?"

"Well, adopted means that you legally take someone else's child and raise him as your own. So for some reason the child being adopted needs a new family. Why do you ask?"

"Because today in Science class we were working on our family trees so that we could trace different characteristics and Jane said hers was hard to do because she was adopted."

"I wonder why her real Mom and Dad didn't keep her," Joanna, the youngest daughter, said thoughtfully.

"I guess we don't know that, Joanna. But we do know that she was loved and given life by one family and now she is loved and cared for by a different family," Mrs. Gooden said quietly.

"Did you ever give one of your children to be adopted? 'Cause I vote we let Tommy be adopted!" piped up Sue. The whole family laughed, knowing it was a joke.

It was quiet at the table for a few minutes as everyone enjoyed their meal.

"Dad, does the Bible talk about adoption?" Paul asked.

"Yes, son, it sure does. You already know that when someone repents of their sin and trusts Jesus as their Lord and Saviour they are born into the family of God, right?"

Heads nodded all around the table. "Well, the Bible also says that in addition to being born into the family of God, we are adopted into His family when we are saved."

"Why do we need to be adopted after we are born into God´s family?" Paul continued.

"Because once you are adopted you cannot legally be abandoned by your adoptive family. Adoption is permanent. So God adopts the new believer to show that He will always belong to God."

"That is really neat," Beth answered. "But what makes people not want their children?"

"Well, that is a hard question to answer because the reasons are often very different. Sometimes the mother and father aren´t married or don´t have jobs and can´t take care of a new baby." Mr. Gooden said.

"Right. And sometimes one or both of the parents get in trouble with the law or even die and so the children need a new family. Did Jane say anything about her biological parents?" Mrs. Gooden added.

"No," Beth said, "I don´t think she wanted to talk about it."

"Well, Beth, then you did good to not ask her any questions. You were sensitive to how she was feeling and that is an important trait to have," Mrs. Gooden replied.

"I just have one more question…what if they can´t find a new family that will love them?" Beth said quietly.

Mrs. Gooden noticed that Beth had tears in her eyes as she asked her question. Gently Mrs. Gooden explained, "Often the children go to a foster home to live, but that is only temporary. Many times the children end up in an orphanage where they stay until they go to college or get a job."

Beth sat quietly, thinking about what she had learned. Finally she said, "I have so much to be thankful for. Thank you, Mom and Dad, for loving me and taking care of me."

Chapter 5

The Gooden Family Learns About the Blind

"Well, that was a first," Mr. Gooden said thoughtfully as he hung up the phone.

"What happened, dear? Is everything ok?" Mrs. Gooden inquired.

"Yes, everything is fine. I just spoke to a lady who has recently moved to town from New York. I think she said her name is Coreen. Anyway, she said she and her husband are looking for a good church and saw our website. They listened to some of the messages and want to come visit the church tomorrow. But here is where it gets interesting. Her husband is blind. He has a braille Bible but it is 18 volumes so he needed to know what Scriptures I was going to preach from so he could bring the right sections."

"Wow – that is really neat," Joanna said. "Maybe some day I can write an article about the blind like I did about the deaf."

"I wonder if he will have one of those white canes," Tommy added.

"There are a lot of things we will learn tomorrow. Let's pray that they make it to church and be sure we make them feel welcome," Mrs. Gooden replied. "But for now, we need to make sure everyone has their clothes and shoes ready for tomorrow."

"I still need to polish my shoes and Dad's and then I will be ready," Paul said. "Then I can read the paper until family devotions."

Each of the Gooden children went their separate ways to make sure they were prepared for the Lord's Day.

That evening as the family gathered to read the Bible together and pray, Mr. Gooden began to read from Proverbs chapter twenty. When he read verse twelve, he stopped and repeated it.

"'The hearing ear and the seeing eye, the Lord hath made even both of them.' Now that is an interesting verse to read after the phone call we had today. You know, children, sometimes when a person loses one of their senses, others become more acute," Mr. Gooden said.

"What is acute?" Tommy asked.

"Acute means more sensitive or refined. So maybe the man we meet tomorrow will be able to hear really well" Mr. Gooden replied.

The next day the Gooden family was thrilled to see the new couple arrive at church. Coreen carried a bag with several volumes of the braille Bible with her and her husband, Marlo, carried his white cane while he held on to her arm for guidance. They told the pastor that Marlo also

knew how to play the guitar and if it would be ok, he would bring it and accompany the musicians as they played. Of course Mr. Gooden was excited about that idea.

That night Marlo arrived carrying his guitar case and white cane. He remembered where they had sat that morning and was able to walk into the church without being guided. When Tommy went to shake his hand, he was surprised that Mr. Marlo remembered his name and recognized his voice. But the big surprise was when the congregation began to sing and the blind man was able to play right along with the pianist and sing the songs without seeing the music or the words! What a good memory God had given him.

As the Gooden family enjoyed their traditional Sunday night snack of popcorn Tommy told the family about how Mr. Marlo remembered his voice after only meeting him that morning. Joanna commented on how he had been able to remember the position of the chairs in the auditorium and find the seat where he had sat in the morning. Every one was content that a new family had visited the church.

Paul finally piped up, "Dad, I helped Mrs. Ketchum carry her bag with the braille Bible in it out to her car. It was really heavy. I was wondering, if they keep coming to the church, maybe we could have a little cart made to store his Bible on so they don´t have to carry it back and forth."

"What a great idea. We can talk to them and see if he can get an extra copy to leave at the church and then make a cart with shelves where he can keep his Bible," Mr. Gooden responded.

"You know, Dad, we learned the verses last night about God making the ears and eyes and He certainly made Mr. Ketchum with extra special hearing since he can't see."

"Very true, Beth. We need to do our best with the talents that God has given us. Marlo certainly has," Mr. Gooden answered.

"With that, I know some children that need to get up early for school tomorrow," Mrs. Gooden said. "Use the bathroom, brush your teeth and soon I will be in to pray with you and tuck you in bed. Tonight we will thank the Lord for the visitors at church and ask Him to help each one of you use your talents for His glory."

Chapter 6

The Gooden Family Gives Their Best

The Gooden children were a bit bleary-eyed as they settled in their chairs for breakfast. All of a sudden Sue´s eyes were round as saucers as her mother put a bowl in front of her.

"Oh Mom!! OATMEAL !" she exclaimed.

"Yes, dear, I know it isn´t your favorite but it is what we have for breakfast so pray and thank the Lord for it and eat quickly. The bus is coming soon," Mrs Gooden replied. "And remember what Luke 10:8b says – eat what is set before you."

Slowly Sue closed her eyes and tried to be thankful. Her brothers and sisters were happily eating their bowls of oatmeal but Sue could barely get the spoon to her mouth. Very softly she said, "I thought we still had eggs in the fridge. This stuff smells bad and I can hardly swallow it."

Mrs. Gooden smothered a grin but answered, "Yes, we do have eggs. But there are just a few and I need them to make the cake for the missionary family that is coming this weekend. If we use the eggs for breakfast we won´t have dessert for their supper. Now, did you leave your rooms presentable for company?"

Each one of the children indicated that their rooms were ready to be used by the missionaries that would spend the weekend at their home.

"Does the family that is coming have children?" asked Joanna.

"Yes, they do. The Keys are missionaries in Brazil and they have several children. I think only the youngest two will be here. Maybe you can think of some questions you would like to ask the children so you can understand more about what their life is like in Brazil," Mrs. Gooden replied.

"I wonder if they like oatmeal," Sue said as she grinned at her mother.

Soon all of the children were brushing their teeth and out the door to wait for the school bus.

All during the day Sue tried to think of what she could ask the missionary's children. She decided to ask them to teach her some words in Portuguese.

That evening after a good meal with the Key family topped off with the special cake Mrs. Gooden had made, the children all got together to ask their questions. Beth asked what their school was like and found out that Brazilian children only go to school a few hours a day. Paul asked what sports they play and learned that soccer is the national sport. Joanna asked about their favorite Brazilian foods and Tommy wanted to know if they had any pets. Sue asked them to teach her how to say several simple things in Portuguese. They had fun all weekend long asking questions and learning all they could about life in Brazil from the Key children.

On Monday morning, as the Gooden children settled around the table for breakfast they chatted about all they had learned about Brazil. Each one of the children except Sue told their parents what questions they had asked and the answers they received. Beth even shared that the Keys´ daughter had said that the cake they had for dessert was her favorite and she was so happy to get to eat it again.

"Thank you, Mom, for saving the eggs so you could make the special cake. It was very important to the missionaries," Tommy said.

Soon Mrs. Gooden put a plate of pancakes on the table. Sue perked up a bit and said, "Luke 10:8b is easier to obey today."

Mr. Gooden asked Sue why she hadn´t shared what she learned over the weekend. Sue explained that she learned several words and phrases like ***oi, tchau, por favor, obrigada*** and ***tudo bem*** but the one she remembered the best was ***mingau de aveia***.

"What is that?" Paul asked.

With a twinkle in her eye, Sue exclaimed, "OATMEAL!"

Chapter 7

The Gooden Family and Father's Day

Tommy's tee ball game had just finished. He was very happy because he had 2 hits and scored 2 runs as well. He also knew that even though they didn't officially keep score, his team had

scored more runs and so that was a win! As he said goodbye to his coach and his teammates, he noticed that one of his buddies, William, was sitting on the bench looking at something in his hand – and he sure didn't look happy.

Tommy went over to William to try to talk to him. "Hey, man, good game!"

William just nodded his head but didn't even look up. Tommy decided to see what William was looking at so he got a little closer and snuck a peak. William was looking at his own baseball card.

"What are you doing with your picture? Gonna give it to a cute girl?" Tommy teased.

William kind of sniffled and said quietly, "I want to give it to my dad for Father's Day but I don't know if I can."

"Well, why can´t you?" Tommy wondered.

"Because my dad is in jail. He did something stupid and had to go to jail. And now Mom is mad at him and I don´t know if she will take me to see him or not. And the rules at the jail mean I can´t take him a gift – not even his favorite candy bar! I mean, tomorrow is Father´s Day and I can´t even see my Dad or take him a present." William was talking so fast that Tommy wasn´t sure he had heard everything but he understood enough to know that William was in a hard spot.

"Maybe you could draw a picture for your dad," Tommy suggested. He really wanted to help but he couldn´t imagine not being with his dad for Father´s Day. "You had that great catch in left field today – draw that for him, since he didn´t get to come. And I will pray that your Mom will take you to see him, ok?"

William seemed to like the idea of making a drawing for his dad. He gathered his things and left the dugout with Tommy.

On the way home Tommy was quiet but the rest of the family was excited. Finally, when his sisters and brother stopped talking his dad asked why he was so quiet. Tommy began to tell the story William had told him.

"And, Dad, his mom is mad and doesn´t want to take him to visit his dad. He really wants to see his dad. Anyway, I was remembering that verse from family devotions the other night. You know, from James. And we talked about the widows but that verse also talks about the fatherless."

"Right, Tommy," Paul said. "I memorized it. James 1:27 says,' Pure religion and undefiled before God and the Father is this, To visit the fatherless and widows in their affliction, and to keep himself unspotted from the world.'"

"So I was thinking that we need to help William, because he is kind of fatherless now. I know we are going to church and we have plans and all for Father´s Day but could you maybe talk to his mom and see if we can help him?"

"I have her phone number, Tommy, so I will give her a call when we get home," Mrs. Gooden answered.

Later that afternoon Mrs. Gooden made the promised phone call. William´s mom said she didn´t realize how much he missed his father and wanted to see him. She said to thank Tommy for talking to him and finding out why he was so sad. Mrs. Gooden invited her to come to church and to have lunch with the Gooden family.

The next morning at church Tommy was thrilled to see William and his mother come through the door. For so long he wanted to bring a friend to Sunday School, and now he had a friend at church! At lunch, however, Tommy realized that William´s mom just couldn´t get the courage up to go to the jail. Both boys were so sad.

"Ma'am, as a pastor, I have been to many jails. And I know what they are like and the rules they have. I know that if you give your permission, I could take your son in to see his father. I think that would be special, since it is Father´s Day," Mr. Gooden said suddenly.

"You would do that? You would give up your special day to take my son to see his father?"

"Of course. The Bible tells us many times that we need to help others when we can. So, I would like to help you and William today," he answered.

Tommy was so thankful for his dad right then. Mr. Gooden took William to see his father and he was even able to give his drawing and his baseball card to his dad. It turned out to be a special day for William and for Tommy as well, because he watched his father obey the Bible.

"When I grow up," Tommy thought, "that is the kind of dad I want to be – one who will help the fatherless in whatever way I can. I am going to memorize James 1:27 and try to live it every day."

Chapter 8

The Gooden Family Learns About Death

"Children, listen while you finish your meal. I have a few things to tell you," Mr. Gooden suddenly said.

The conversations around the table ceased quickly and all eyes looked at their father. This happened so rarely that they knew something important was about to occur.

"As you know, our beloved Mrs. Hart has not been doing well. She is 95 years old and her body is just wearing out. She has been a faithful prayer warrior and member of the church for years. I want us to go as a family to visit her one more time so that we can sing her favorite songs, pray with her and thank her for praying for us. As soon as dishes are washed I want you each to get cleaned up and into church clothes so we can go visit her. I spoke with her daughter and they are expecting us in about an hour."

For a few minutes it was very quiet at the Gooden table. Each one was lost in their own thoughts and memories of Mrs. Hart. Pretty soon their attention turned back to their plates and finishing their supper. More than one sniffle was heard as the children excused themselves and began to clear the table and wash dishes.

As they drove the short distance to Mrs. Hart's house different ones began to share their memories of her.

"I remember unloading all that wood that was sent from New York so we could build the church building and carrying it to her backyard to store it," Paul said.

"I remember asking her at prayer meeting how she was feeling and she told me she was tired because she had mowed her lawn that morning. Of course she was tired!" Sue exclaimed. "She was nearly 90 years old and still out there pushing her mower around!"

"I remember her bringing vegetables from her garden to people at church. She sure was a hard worker," Joana added.

"Yes," Mrs. Gooden replied. "When Mrs. Hart was a young girl her mother died and she stopped going to school so she could take care of her younger brothers and sisters and let her dad continue working on the farm. She learned to work hard from a very young age."

"Children, we are here. Please remember to speak loudly and slowly when you speak to Mrs. Hart but otherwise we need you to sit quietly," Mr. Gooden advised.

As they walked into the living room where a hospital bed had been arranged the children moved in a group to sit on the sofa. Their father read a few of Mrs. Hart´s favorite passages and watched as her face lit up when she heard their mother´s beautiful voice singing "In the Garden"…

I come to the garden alone,

While the dew is still on the roses,

And the voice I hear falling on my ear,

The Son of God discloses…

 All the children and Mr. Gooden joined in on the chorus…

And He walks with me, and He talks with me,

And He tells me I am His own,

And the joy we share as we tarry there,

None other, has ever, known!

Soon the children thanked the precious lady for all she had done for them and for her prayers and they headed back outside to the family van.

"I think that is the hardest thing I have ever done," Beth choked out as tears ran down her face.

"Yes, dear, these things are hard to face. But one thing we know is that if we are saved we will see Mrs. Hart again in heaven." Mrs. Gooden reached back to squeeze Beth´s hand as she spoke.

A few days later the phone call telling of Mrs. Hart´s death caused another round of memory sharing and tears in the Gooden home.

"One thing is for sure," Paul said, "we will miss her prayers. She prayed so faithfully for our church and our missionaries that we need to step up and pray more."

As Paul spoke, Mr. Gooden nodded his head and then added, "That is a challenge all of us need to take on. We can never pray too much!"

Chapter 9

The Gooden Family Celebrates Thanksgiving

"That was a good meal, Mama, may I please be excused?" Sue asked.

"Not yet," Mr. Gooden answered quickly. "I have something I want to talk to you all about.

Sue settled back into her seat and put her plate back on the table. The children looked at each other quickly and then back at their father. He didn´t usually keep them after a meal to chat so they were curious about what he wanted to say.

"I was thinking about the verse we have learned about taking care of the orphans and fatherless," Mr. Gooden began. "I really want us to invite some of these people to share Thanksgiving with us this year. I was thinking about some of the people from the church or our neighborhood that don´t have family and will be alone this year."

"We won´t go to Grandma´s this year?" Joanna asked softly.

"No. I think this year we ought to look for ways to serve others," Mr. Gooden replied.

Eyes twinkling, Sue quickly piped up, "Well, we always have to rake Grandma's leaves when we go there, so at least we won't have to do that this year."

Everyone giggled but soon sobered up thinking about not seeing their family. Each one of the children knew they would miss seeing their aunts and uncles, cousins and grandparents and it was hard to think about missing out on the fun.

"Who do you want to invite, dear?" Mrs. Gooden asked.

"I don't know. I thought we could think about it and pray about it together as a family and see how the Lord leads. Let's talk again during Sunday dinner."

That week during family devotions the Goodens prayed for the Lord to show them who they could help on Thanksgiving. Each one of the family members thought of different ones they could invite. Attitudes began to change from sadness about not seeing their family to understanding why their parents wanted to help others.

The days passed quickly and soon they were all seated around the dining room table eating a wonderful meal of roast beef, mashed potatoes and gravy, green beans and salad.

Mr. Gooden soon began the conversation they were all waiting for. "Who should we invite to join us for Thanksgiving?"

"I was thinking of our new neighbors, since they just moved here and don't have any family in the area. Their son, Ethan, is Paul's age," Mrs. Gooden said.

"I wanted to invite William and his mother but he said they are going to his aunt´s house," Tommy added.

"What about the neighbor across the street? He seems to be alone and we know his wife isn´t well so she can´t cook. It might really help them and since they aren´t Christians maybe we can show some of God´s love and mercy to them," Joanna said.

"That is so kind of you to think of them. We can invite them but if she doesn´t feel well enough to come we can offer to send a plate over to them," Mrs. Gooden replied. "Go over there tomorrow and invite them and we´ll see which way works best for them. And tonight, I will call Carrie when she gets home from work and ask if they would like to spend the day with us."

Both Joanna and Mrs. Gooden invited the neighbors, who were amazed by the invitation and said they would love to join the Goodens for Thanksgiving.

The morning of Thanksgiving was full of baking and cooking, cleaning and vacuuming. The older girls got out the decorations and put the pilgrims in the center of the table before helping their mother to put the finishing touches on the meal.

The guests arrived and everyone crowded into the dining room and around the table. Before praying for the meal Mr. Gooden gave each person the opportunity to say something for which they are thankful. The little neighbor lady, Mrs. Jones, said, "I am thankful for being invited here today. Turkey and dressing is my husband´s favorite meal and I knew I just wouldn´t have the strength to make it for him today."

That day the Gooden children learned that putting others´ needs ahead of their own was an important life lesson.

Chapter 10

The Gooden Family Shares Their Dreams

"May Paul and I please split the last hot dog?"

Thomas caught the amused look that passed between his mom and dad at his question. "We are growing boys and we each have a hollow leg that needs filled up," he quipped.

"Sure son, have the last hot dog," Mrs. Gooden replied. "I dream about the day that your hollow legs fill up."

The family all sat around a picnic table at their favorite park. Everyone chuckled at Mrs. Gooden´s chagrin with her sons.

"That is an interesting topic for us to chat about," Mr. Gooden said. "What kinds of dreams do you children have for your future? I think it would be fun if each of us shared a dream. Honey you can share another one if you choose," he winked at his wife.

"Oh, that is easy," Tommy perked up. "Some day I want to have money to go to the grocery store and choose whatever I want!! That would be amazing!!"

"I want to grow up and get married and have a dozen children…and I want to be a teacher too!" Joanna piped up. "I know that is two dreams but they are kind of the same – I want to always be around children, both my own and others."

"Well, you know that to be a teacher you will have to study a lot," Mr. Gooden advised. "What about you, Paul?"

"I think I might want to tag along when Tommy goes to the grocery store," he quipped before getting serious. "No, I would love to own a red sports car some day. I saw a Buick Reatta the other day that was really neat. Of course when I get married and have a family that will change but I think it would be fun while I am still single."

"I guess if we are going in order of age, I am next," Sue said. Everyone saw that suspicious twinkle in her eye that warned them something outrageous was coming. "I want to be a researcher."

"What do you mean?" Beth asked.

"You know how Dad always says 'Someone should do a survey about that' so I figure with all of his ideas I would never run out of work!" The whole family chuckled and then waited for her real answer.

"I would love to start a foundation. Like the kind that gives money to charities and stuff. But I would want to be able to support missionaries and missionary projects."

"You seem to have thought a lot about this," Mrs. Gooden replied.

"I have. And I even have a name for it…it would be The Widow's Mite. So, Beth, what is one of your dreams?"

"Ever since I learned about adoption I have wondered about orphanages. I think I would love to visit an orphanage some day and maybe even work with orphans. I love children and want some of my own, but would even pray about adopting, too. And what about you, Mama?"

"My dream, besides eradicating hollow leg syndrome, is from the book of Third John. Verse four says, 'I have no greater joy than to hear that my children walk in truth.' My greatest dream is to see each one of you grow up and walking with the Lord. I love to hear your dreams and it will be fun to see how many come true, but even if they don't and you are serving the Lord I will be more than happy."

"Honey, I totally agree with you," Mr. Gooden said. "And I have a dream that will hopefully go hand in hand with your mother's dream. I have prayed about this for a long time and I think today is the day to share it with everyone. My dream is to be able to take each one of you on a

trip to visit a different mission field. I want you to learn to eat different foods and appreciate other cultures. I want you to have a burden for people that have never heard the gospel. So, let's begin to pray about this as a family and see what the Lord allows us to do."

That announcement caused quite a bit of excitement and conversation as the children cleaned up from their picnic and scattered to play. Mr. Gooden sat back and reached for his wife's hand before saying, "The Lord has been good to our family. I can hardly wait to see what other adventures He has in store for us."

ABOUT THE AUTHOR

Robynn Reno is a career missionary who has served the Lord in Brazil and Venezuela. Her favorite thing to do is teach God's Word, whether it be to juvenile delinquents, street children, prisoners, youth groups, Sunday schools, women's Bible studies or just one-on-one. She has written and translated many Bible studies for use in the ministry. In order to better equip herself and others for ministry, Robynn completed her Doctor of Religious Education degree in 2006. In her spare time Robynn loves to read or watch home improvement videos from the comfort of her hammock.